CARLOS
The Street Boy Who Found a Home

Marcos Carpenter

Photographs by
Ben Alex

A LION BOOK
Tring · Batavia · Sydney

4

It was late afternoon in São Paulo, Brazil's largest city. Rush hour traffic inched along, bumper to bumper. Carlos was already at the busy crossroads where he sold flowers every afternoon.

When the traffic lights turned red, Carlos went from car to car. He showed the flowers and offered them at a cheap price. If he didn't hurry out of the way when the lights turned green, he would get run over. It was a dangerous job, and Carlos hated it. But if he didn't earn a pocket full of money each day, he and his Uncle Bento would go hungry.

'Get out of here!' yelled an angry driver. 'Go home!' But Carlos had no home. At night he slept in a tiny shack in one of São Paulo's slums, called *favelas*. Sometimes his Uncle Bento slept there, too, when he wasn't out drinking.

It was almost dark when Carlos sold the last bunch of roses. With the money safe in his pocket, he started across the park toward the *favela* where he lived. But Carlos didn't look forward to getting back. It was late, and Uncle Bento would be angry because he had to wait so long to go to the bar.

'Where's the money?' Uncle Bento demanded when Carlos came back. Carlos reached deep into his pocket, then held out the small handful of *cruzado*, Brazilian banknotes. Uncle Bento snatched them away and left the shack. He needed Carlos' money to buy drink.

For supper, Carlos found some stale scraps of leftover *mandioca*, a starchy white root that tastes like potatoes when cooked. Then he laid a blanket on the bed, and slumped down alongside Uncle Bento's empty bottles.

'If only mother hadn't died,' Carlos thought to himself. 'If only my father had never gone off and left us. But now he is dead, too.' That night Carlos dreamed that his parents were still alive.

When Carlos awoke early the next morning, he found himself lying on the floor covered by a dirty blanket. Uncle Bento was snoring on the bed beside him. Another empty bottle of drink lay on the floor.

Carlos got up, stretched, and put on the same ragged clothes. He took the last piece of dry bread, then decided to go into the city centre to beg some more food. He would not have to be back until the middle of the afternoon, when his uncle would arrive with more flowers for him to sell.

Carlos went to the underground station and rode down the escalator. But he had no money for a ticket. When no one was looking, he crawled under the ticket barrier. Carlos knew it wasn't honest.

The train was crowded with all sorts of people. There was a tall blond man, several black women, three Chinese schoolgirls, and many people with skin the colour of Carlos'. He remembered something he had heard Uncle Bento say: '*O Brasil é de todos nós!*' 'Brazil belongs to the world!' Carlos' uncle had told him that most people in Brazil had originally come from other countries all over the world. 'That's why there's no such thing as a typical Brazilian,' he had said.

The people on the train wore nice clean clothes and looked as though they were going off to important jobs. Carlos spotted a boy his age wearing an expensive track suit and carrying a tennis racket. When the boy saw Carlos looking at him, he stuck his tongue out.

Carlos' face turned red. It seemed as though everyone was staring at his torn clothes and dirty hair. When the train went round a sharp bend, a young woman lost her balance and leaned against him. She looked with disgust at Carlos, and brushed off her skirt where it had touched him.

Carlos felt as though the entire world hated him.

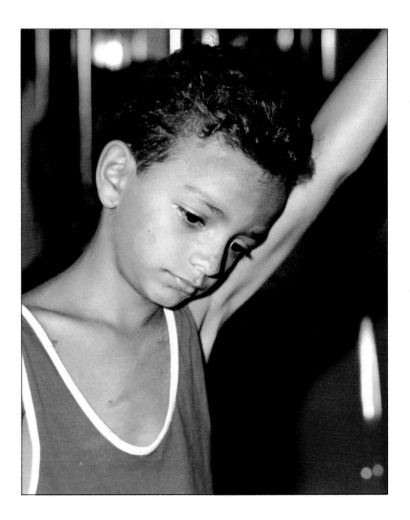

When the train finally pulled into the Praca da Sé station in a large park, Carlos got off quickly. He was glad to be away from the glares and stares of all those people. As he came out of the underground station into the sunshine, he forgot about the boy with the tennis racket.

Carlos spotted a group of boys like himself—ragged street kids—playing in the fountain. Carlos jumped in with them. He swam and splashed until an impatient policeman shooed them all away.

There were hundreds of people in the park, all hurrying off in different directions. Several disabled people sat on newspapers on the ground, begging for money. 'Take pity, for the love of God,' they pleaded. Other people gathered around street pedlars who sold everything you could ever imagine—socks, cheap watches, lottery tickets, stomach medicine and lots of other things. Still others simply sat around, enjoying the sun.

Just then a gang of noisy street kids approached Carlos.

'Hey, look at that man sitting on the bench over there,' said one of them. 'His wallet is in his shirt pocket. We're going to sneak up behind him and knock him on the head. Then we'll grab the wallet. Want to help? We'll split the money later, OK?'

Carlos wanted the money, but he didn't want to hurt the man or rob him. 'No. Just leave the guy alone,' he replied.

'*Medroso!* Chicken!' they taunted. The boys made fun of Carlos. Then they turned and walked toward the man sitting on the bench.

The man looked up at the gang of boys for just a second, then he went back to reading his newspaper. Suddenly one of the boys dashed around the bench and distracted the man's attention. Another boy snatched his wallet. They ran across the park and disappeared into the crowd.

'I can't believe it!' Carlos said to himself. 'They really did it!'

A crowd began to gather. The man pointed straight at Carlos and yelled, 'There's one of them! He's one of the thieves!'

Carlos' heart began to beat wildly. 'He thinks *I* did it!' he said out loud. Carlos wanted to run away, but his feet wouldn't move. Suddenly a large hand grabbed the neck of his tee-shirt and nearly lifted him off the ground. A plain-clothes policeman! The man pushed him into the back of a van.

Before long Carlos found himself at the police station. Nothing like this had ever happened to him before. He began to tremble from head to foot. He had heard that street boys were sometimes given beatings at the police headquarters.

'All right, where's the old man's money?' the policeman demanded. He gave Carlos a shove on the shoulder.

'But it wasn't me!' Carlos whimpered. He shrunk back against the wall. After a few more questions Carlos was pushed back into the van and driven away. He was taken to a camp for boys in trouble with the law.

As Carlos walked through the heavy iron gates of the camp, he shuddered with fear. Everyone inside looked tough and mean.

'What did you do to get sent here?' asked a tall dark boy with a scar on his chest.

'Nothing!' Carlos replied. The boy just laughed at him.

Carlos found out that he had to sleep on an old mattress in the same room as eighty other boys. He was going to have to sleep beside thieves, murderers, and drug pushers. His stomach was in knots.

Three days later, Carlos felt even worse. These street kids didn't like him any more than the well-dressed boy on the underground. Besides that, a couple of big, tough kids had threatened to beat him up. 'You're a coward,' they told him. 'You won't even admit what you did wrong! You're going to get some trouble from us!'

Later that morning one of the guards announced that a church group from the city would give a puppet show that afternoon.

'And if there's any trouble,' he warned, 'you'll be sorry. I mean it!'

A large group of kids gathered to watch the puppet show. It was led by a pretty woman called Tia Noeme. The boys started to whistle, but most of them listened. When it was over Tia Noeme sang a song for them. She had a lovely voice. To Carlos, she seemed so gentle and caring.

'No matter how bad you've been or how many people you've hurt, Jesus still loves you,' she told the boys.

Carlos thought, 'Can anybody actually love *me*?'

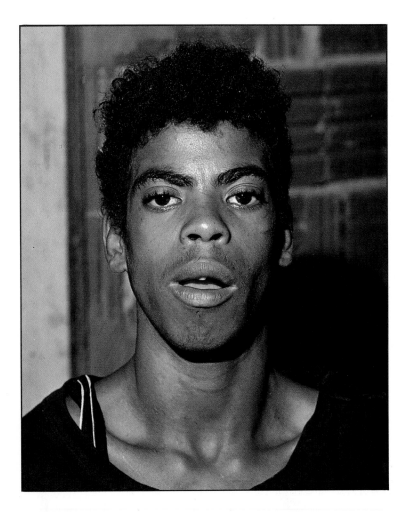

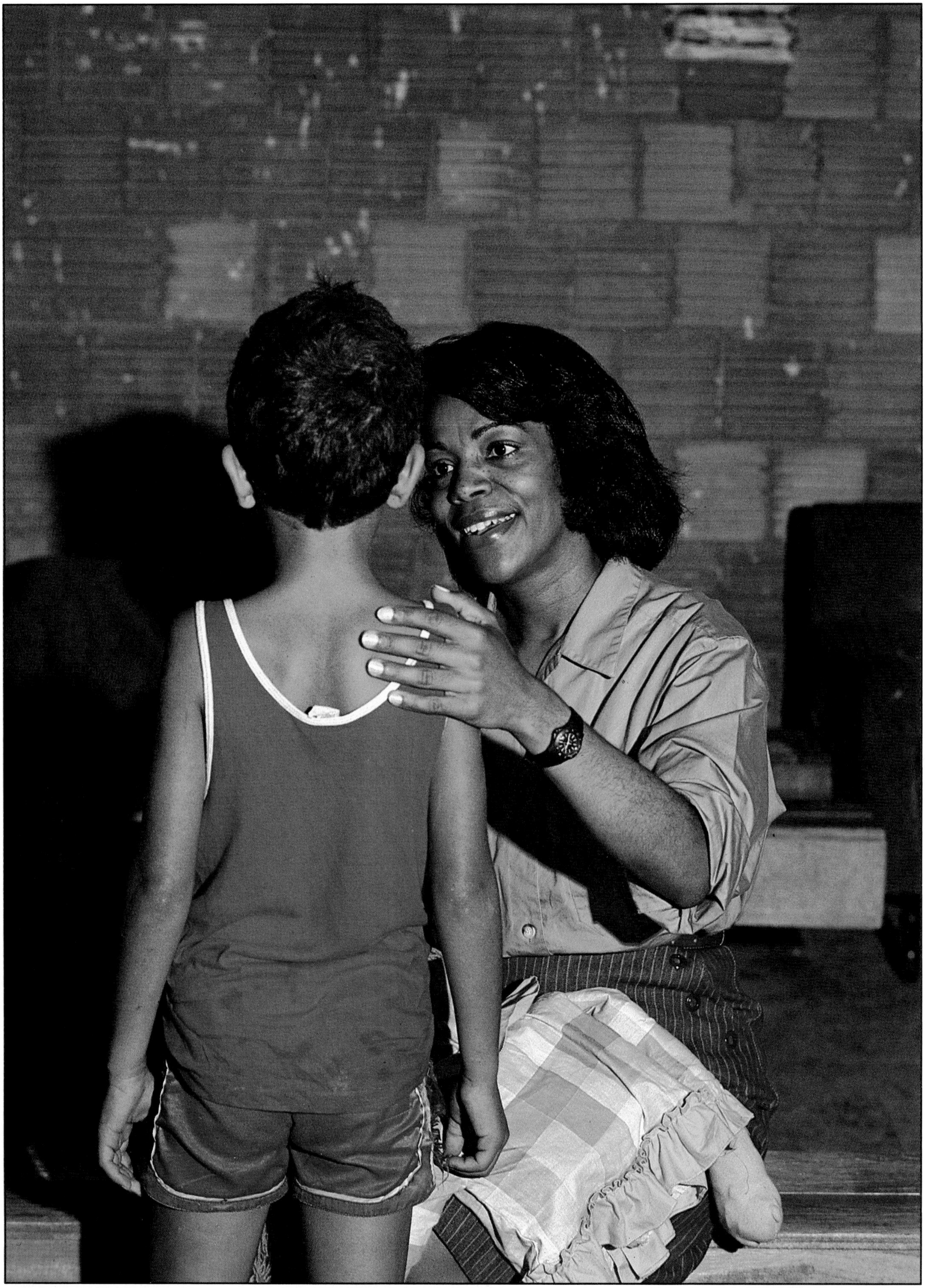

Carlos waited until most of the other boys had left, then he hung around, hoping to talk to Tia Noeme. She noticed him, and knelt down to talk to him.

'What's your name?' she asked. 'Carlos,' he whispered, and lowered his head. Suddenly, tears began rolling down his face. Carlos told Tia Noeme everything—about his mother who had died when he was four years old, about his dead father, about Uncle Bento, about selling flowers. He started to tell her that he had not beaten up the man in the park.

Tia Noeme didn't laugh at him like the others did. 'I'm not sure I can help you get out of here,' she said. 'But I am sure that Jesus will care for you. He wants you to trust in him.'

Tia Noeme sat down with Carlos and told him more about Jesus. 'Jesus is the Son of God,' she said. 'He came to earth to save us. He gave his life so that we might be forgiven for all the wrong things we have done.'

Carlos remembered all the bad things he had done. He had crawled under the ticket barrier at the underground station without paying many times. He had cheated flower-buyers out of their correct change. And sometimes, he had hated his Uncle Bento.

Tia Noeme broke into Carlos' thoughts. 'Jesus will forgive you for everything if you ask him to. He loves you. Do you want to give your life to Jesus?'

Carlos didn't know what to say. He knew he needed someone stronger than himself to turn to. But something inside him kept saying, 'No, no, not now.'

Tia Noeme understood Carlos' struggle. She prayed, 'Lord Jesus, give Carlos the courage to accept you and to trust you.'

She turned to Carlos and said, 'Remember, you can pray at any time. Just talk to Jesus as if he were your very best friend. And I'll be praying for you, too.'

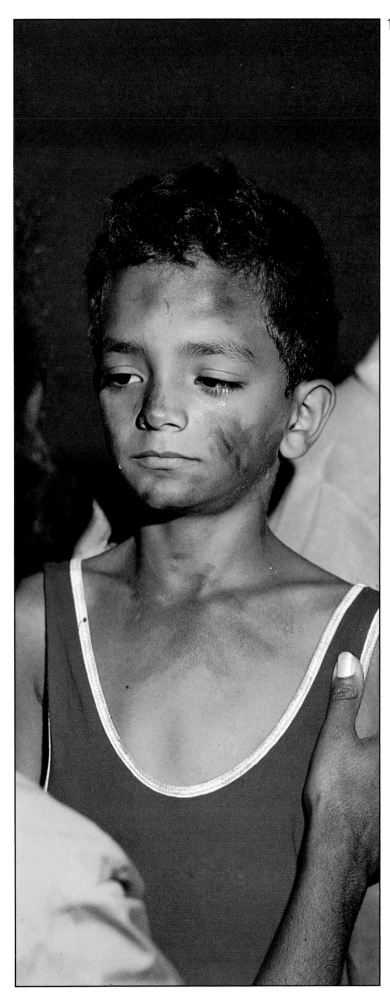

That night as Carlos lay down on the hard mattress alongside all the other boys, he thought about Tia Noeme's prayer. He wished he had prayed while he still had the chance.

He closed his eyes and whispered, 'Jesus, I'm all alone. Help me, somehow. Forgive me and help me trust in you.'

Then Carlos fell asleep. Little did he know that someone who loved him was very close . . . as close as his own heart.

'Carlos! *Acorda!* Wake up!'

Carlos sat up straight and rubbed his eyes. It was the early morning guard shouting in his ear. 'Get up!' he repeated. 'You're lucky. The man in the park found the real muggers and admitted you were innocent. Those boys will be taking your place here. You're free!'

Carlos could hardly believe his ears. He jumped off the mattress and ran outside. He had to wait at the camp office for an official document to be signed.

The director of the boys' camp looked down at Carlos. 'I don't ever want to see you back here,' he warned.

'Don't worry,' smiled Carlos. 'I won't be back!'

Then the iron gates swung open. Carlos was free to go. The air outside seemed cleaner and fresher than before. He started the long walk back to the *favela*.

By late morning Carlos arrived at the lower entrance of the *favela*. As he passed through the same old gate, he could smell the terrible stench of the open sewers. He held his nose and started up the hill toward Uncle Bento's shack.

Carlos was not sure what to expect from Uncle Bento. Would he be happy to see Carlos? Would he be angry? Carlos knew that if Uncle Bento had been drinking the night before, he would still be asleep.

As Carlos approached the shack, he noticed the door was open. That meant Uncle Bento was awake. Then a woman he had never seen before appeared in the doorway.

'Where's Uncle Bento?' asked Carlos.

'Who are you?' the woman demanded, her hands on her hips.

Carlos told her who he was.

'Well, listen,' she explained, 'I don't know why you haven't heard, but your uncle was in a fight last week at the bar. He died of knife wounds. Now this place is mine! And I don't want any kids around! So get out!'

'But what about—' Carlos began. His face was pale.

'I said get out!' the woman screeched.

Carlos stared after the woman as she went back into the shack. Then her words began to sink in. Carlos walked back down the hill with an aching heart. There was no one else he could go to, and no one he could live with. He felt numb and sick, thinking about Uncle Bento.

'Now what will I do?' he wondered. 'I have no money, no place to sleep, no way to get flowers to sell. Why? Why?' The questions tumbled through his mind. He walked and walked, remembering Tia Noeme and the promise she had made to pray for him. Wasn't Jesus supposed to help him? Carlos didn't understand why Jesus had allowed him to be poor and homeless and hungry.

'I just want to be an ordinary kid,' he said to himself, choking back tears. 'A kid with a mum or a dad, or maybe even both, and all of us with enough to eat.'

Before long, Carlos was in the city centre, surrounded by tall buildings. A thick haze of afternoon pollution hung in the air, along with the heavy smell of exhaust fumes from the traffic. People rushed by him in all directions. But nobody noticed him. Nobody cared.

The sky had turned dark and cloudy. Big drops of rain began to fall. Carlos sat down on the steps of the old cathedral. The cold wind made goose-pimples come up on his arms. He shivered in the grey, lonely afternoon.

After a while the rain stopped. As Carlos got up, he could smell the aroma of something delicious wafting through the air. He began to feel very hungry. But there would be nothing delicious for him to eat.

He walked down a dark, narrow alley until he came to the back door of a restaurant. Several rubbish bags filled with scraps of old food lay outside. Carlos brushed away the flies, then pulled out an apple core and a boiled pig's ear that had been used to flavour a black-bean dish called *feijoada*. He ate quickly and hurried back to the street. The scraps of food tasted awful, but at least they filled his stomach.

The sun set and the evening air grew chilly. Carlos looked for an old newspaper to use as a blanket. After walking around for a while, he decided to lie down and sleep on the front steps of a bank. He tried to find shelter from the wind and lay down. He lay down on the newspaper he had found. As he lay there shivering on the hard steps, large tears rolled down his cheeks.

The noise of the city traffic finally stopped. Carlos was still lying awake, shivering. The cold cut right through his bones. Suddenly he heard something different from the other night sounds. He listened. It sounded almost like . . . singing! It sounded like the kind of music Tia Noeme sang at the boys' camp.

Carlos sat up, throwing the newspaper aside. He ran to the corner and looked down the empty street. In the middle of the block, on the other side of the road, he saw a small, brightly-lit building between two skyscrapers. Carlos hurried across the street. As he approached the door he thought he heard the same song that Tia Noeme had sung.

Carlos peered through the crack between the open doors. A group of children were singing, and there was Tia Noeme leading them! Carlos was filled with happiness. He opened the door eagerly and joined the children on the front row.

Carlos listened carefully as Tia Noeme told the children about the love of Jesus. When she had finished, Carlos hurried up to Tia Noeme. Her eyes sparkled with excitement when she recognized him.

'How did you get out of the boys' camp?' she asked.

Carlos told her all about it. Then he told her that Uncle Bento was dead. 'I'm all alone now,' he said.

'Well, you've come to the right place,' replied Tia Noeme. 'This is a place for children just like you. We have food and beds for street kids without homes or families of their own. We want you to stay with us. You belong here, Carlos!'

Carlos' smile got bigger and bigger. 'Thank you,' he said.

One morning a few weeks later, Tia Noeme came hurrying to find Carlos. 'Come into my office,' she said. 'There are some people here who want to meet you.'

Carlos came in and saw a kind-looking man and a woman.

'Carlos,' Tia Noeme began. 'This is Reinaldo and Maria Souza. They have no children, and have come here because they would like to adopt a homeless boy to be their son. I have told them all about you.'

Carlos looked at the man and woman. They were smiling at him. Their eyes were full of hope. For a moment Carlos remembered all the times he had cried because he wished he had at least one parent. He looked at Tia Noeme, then at the Souzas once more.

Carlos spent the afternoon with Reinaldo and Maria, talking and walking around town. They bought Carlos a big hamburger and the best milkshake he ever had. Then they returned to Tia Noeme. Carlos told her he'd made up his mind. He wanted to go home with them.

'Great!' was all Reinaldo could say. Tears of happiness streamed down Maria's face. She hugged Carlos. And he hugged her back.

'I know you'll be very happy,' said Tia Noeme, wiping tears from her eyes.

Carlos climbed into the back seat of the Souza's car and as they rode along, Maria told him all about their own lives. Carlos had never met anyone in his life who seemed more loving or caring.

They continued to drive on and on, out of the city of São Paulo and into the country. At last, Carlos drifted off to sleep.

When he woke up, they were pulling into the drive. Carlos saw a real house with a chimney and a garden and windows of glass!

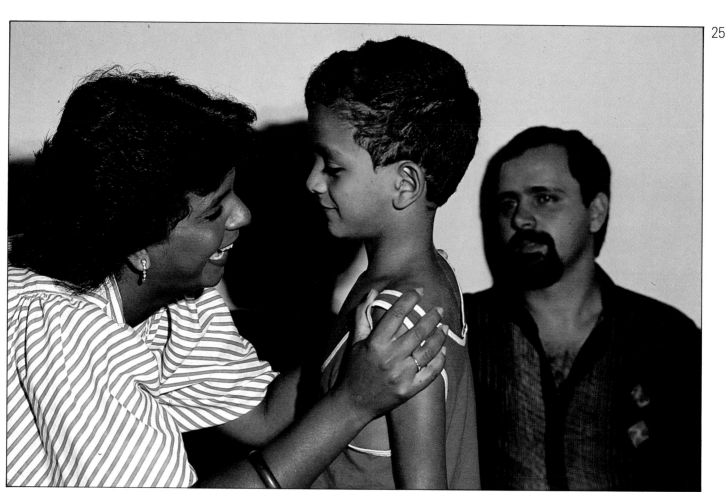

26

When they were inside, Maria showed him his very own room.

'We want you to feel at home, Carlos. Everything in this room is yours.' Maria leaned down and kissed him on the cheek. 'I'm so glad you're here,' she whispered.

During supper, Reinaldo told Carlos, 'You can begin going to school after the summer holidays.'

The next morning Carlos had a big breakfast. It was the first time in his life he had ever eaten so much at one time. There was coffee mixed with hot milk, French bread, papaya slices, ham, cheese, and Carlos' favourite—thick slabs of a gooey, dark spread made from the tasty guava fruit. He had never tasted anything so wonderful.

Just as he was finishing, the doorbell rang. Maria opened the door, and Carlos saw a group of boys in shorts and soccer boots. One of them was holding a football.

'We heard there was a new kid living here,' said the tallest boy. 'Can he come and play with us?'

Carlos' eyes lit up. Like most Brazilian boys, he loved football. He had played it often in the *favela*, using a stuffed paper bag for a ball.

Once on the field, Carlos kicked the ball right past his opponents and into the goal.

'Well done, Carlos!' shouted his new friends.

The next day was Sunday. 'Carlos! *Acorda!* Wake up!'

Carlos sat up with a shock. For a moment he thought he was back in the boys' camp. But when he saw Reinaldo, a smile of relief crossed his face.

Reinaldo said, 'We're going to church today. You'll make even more friends and learn about how God answers prayer.'

'Oh, I already know all about that!' Carlos replied. 'You are the answer to my prayers!'

A few weeks later Reinaldo asked if Carlos would like to drive into the city with him for the day.

'Yeah!' Carlos shouted. He loved riding in the car almost as much as he loved playing football.

At the end of the day, as they were leaving São Paulo and heading for home once more, Reinaldo stopped the car at a set of traffic lights. A sad-looking boy approached their car, holding several bunches of roses. Carlos' heart sank. The boy was wearing a torn shirt and had dirty hair. Angry drivers were yelling at him. Reinaldo gave the boy some money for the roses.

Carlos watched the boy head toward other cars. He knew what it felt like to sell roses in heavy traffic, to be hungry and homeless and afraid all the time.

'I wonder where that boy will sleep tonight,' Carlos said to Reinaldo.

That night as Carlos lay in bed he remembered the boy selling flowers.

'He is just like me,' he thought. 'But everything's changed for me. Lord Jesus, why do some children have to suffer, while others have so much? Thank you for giving me a home and a mum and dad. Give the boy with the flowers what he needs tonight, and let him hear about Jesus too.'

Then Carlos fell fast asleep.